I0477308

How to Master Day Trading Selection for Beginners
Easy and Fast Advanced Trading for High Profitability
Ricardo Calca
If you enjoyed learning the information in this book... you may
also be interested in...
other titles by Ricardo Calca
If you have been helped by the information in this book please
take a minute by letting me know how it helped you by leaving a
review on the bookseller where you purchased you book.
I am always interested to know how my readers are doing and
what successes they are having in the markets.
Wishing you a profitable day!
Ricardo Calca

Who I wrote this book for

I have written this book for all brand new traders who are just getting into trading and have zero or very little experience yet. This book will give you the necessary information you need from an insider perspective. How you choose to use this information is completely up to you though. If you are already trading, you are consistently profitable on a daily basis that's awesome and you should continue to do what is working for you, the information in this book will be elementary for you.

If you have zero experience the information in this book is worth its weight in gold because it is given to you all in one place at one time. It would take you years to figure out how to play with and trade with the smart money in an environment where people have a "kill everyone" mentality when it comes to making money with money. Make no mistake *you* as a brand new trader are the one who pays the professionals in the market. Until you have an edge and can trade with real money in the live market and be consistently profitable on a daily basis you will be the one who is lining the professionals and the smart money's accounts.

Ask yourself this question then, do I want be the one who is paying *or* do I want to be the one who *gets* paid? If you do what it says in this book you will have a great chance at developing a winning edge needed to work in the live markets with real money every day. If you don't then *you don't*! All that really happens in the market is a transfer of account from one traders account to another's.

Brand new traders all make the same mistakes over and over because they don't know any better. They do what everyone else is doing and study what everyone else is studying thus they have the same results and failures as everyone else. Don't be *that* trader! If you can just take the time to read this information in this first book in the series, let it sink in and then continue on your educational journey you will have done yourself a huge favor and also begun to give yourself the needed edge to succeed in this business.

Hey listen you can trade demo all you want and I suggest you do only until you are 100% proficient with your chosen trading platform whatever it is. It is the only way to become good at placing entries. Just remember though, that what you are doing on the demo platform of your software is not being transmitted to the live market and no one is on the other side of the trade you are executing.

Always remember that for everyone who has a winning trade someone has to have lost. When you execute a trade in the live market someone has to be on the other side of the trade to give you an order. It is honestly the best business in the world to be in as far as I am concerned but that's just me. It is nothing more than supply and demand at work and the only way the live markets work. I will have a link to where you can study supply and demand later in the book and also a link to a supply and demand trading learning thread that is the best on the internet and is also *free*.

You can learn everything you need to know about supply and demand day trading for free and then use all of the money that you would be spending on all those fancy trading courses and trading systems or indicators that you *don't need* for your start initial risk capital to work with in the live market.

Once you have gotten used to your trading software and platform I encourage you to move right into the live market and use real money to trade with. I will tell you why and how right now. As I said on demo no one is on the other side of your execution on demo thus you cannot make any real money. When you feel the time is right you can open up a real money account at your broker of choice and use your account to place trades in the live market in a micro Forex contract or a micro-cap stock position.

By doing this you will be able to get a feel of what the real money market environment is like both *good* and *bad*. There are going to be some unfavorable outcomes in the live markets that cause you to lose some money, it's a given and a known fact so there should be no surprise if and when it happens to *you*.

Trading real money on a micro size level will enable you to begin to develop the mental ability to be in the live market with the sharks who are circling you and are eyeing your account capital like a piece of prey. You must be able to experience what the live market environment is like without exposing a great amount of your hard earned money to the sharks.

Using real money right away will also let you see if your rule based plan you have composed will be sustainable and profitable in the live market environment. You only need to use a *small* amount of money to test out your plan. This is a huge mistake brand new trader's make because they have not done all the required research into all the possible methods of trading the live markets. This one mistake can cause a brand new trader to lose all of their money in the first few months of their trading career and make it a very short endeavor.

There is no need for that to happen *and* you can be making a little bit of *real money* while you are doing your testing provided you have composed a solid rule based plan that has given you a money making edge over all the other competition you will be working against in the live market.

You need to have put *all* the probabilities of having a positive financial outcome in your favor *before* you step foot in the live market trading a full size contract in any asset class. You absolutely need to know what is working and what is not working and trading real money on a micro account will enable you to see this crucial information *before* you make any mistakes that can be expensive and perhaps end your trading career and business before you ever get it going. Don't be *that* trader!

What all beginners must know when they start out

The decision you are making to get into the day trading business is one of the most important decisions of your life. Getting into this business and becoming good enough at it to make a comfortable living from it will test your being to the very core. This is one business that will expose every flaw you have and then some. There is no hiding in this business, and there are people in the business *already* who know you better than you know yourself at this juncture and they are going to take complete advantage of your every flaw until you "*get it*" and become a consistently profitable professional whose using a rule based plan every day.

Make no mistake the live markets are full of people who will walk over the smoking wreckage you're blown up account to get paid and not think twice about it. It is just business as usual in the for them every day and should you not take the time think about what you are doing and rush to learn anything in this business only one thing will happen. Smoking wreckage!

Picture yourself throwing all your startup capital into the bon fire at the party you'll throw for yourself for starting your new trading business up and watch it burn up in smoke and flames right before your very eyes. You smell that? That's all your money burning up because you went to fast or did not learn what to do the right way from the first day of your business.

Let me paint a couple of different pictures for you right up front so you can get a picture of what it will be like going in the live markets without a rule based plan and unprepared or even underprepared in *your* mind. This will give you an idea of what can happen by not using a rule based plan in your trading and investing business.

Think of yourself on a nice vacation down in beautiful Australia and you are out sport fishing somewhere around the Great Barrier Reef.

Now you are preparing to set your line but need to get your chum (bait) out first and as you are working on the chum you accidently cut a very deep gash into your leg around your Femoral artery, *and* just at *the* moment you do *that* a rogue wave hits the boat and knocks you *and* the chum bucket overboard and into the water. Now you are the water bleeding profusely *with the chum* and the 21 foot great white sharks that frequent the area you are fishing in. It is said that great white sharks can smell blood in the water for 1000 nautical miles and be in the area in a nanosecond. You can finish this one however *you* like but the sharks win.

The second one is real easy. Imagine you have some huge cajones and you decide you are going play Russian roulette with a loaded revolver that's *fully* loaded. As the song says "click click BOOM"! Only *you* are the one who is going to get FUBAR. That's what you'll be doing by going in the live market unprepared and without a plan. You can kid yourself all you want and say "it will never happen to me" however trust me it will. Later on in this book there is some information on mistakes that *all* brand new investors and traders make. I encourage you to pay attention to it closely.

While these examples may seem harsh to you if you are brand new and have zero experience and are looking for information to get you started in the trading and investing business just remember them when you are screwing around on demo doing all the kooky stuff you *will* do. Demo is where you can do all that crazy stuff you will try, like trading 20 cars on crude oil or gold with no plan. Get it *alllll* out of your system in demo though because the sharks are waiting for you in the live market. The sharks just *might* hand you a loaded revolver so be prepared.

The harsh reality of the market is that there are people in there who are smarter than you, have waaaaaaaay more money than you, have better algo than you and are trying to take your money and transfer it from your account to theirs. Are you going to *let* that happen? By now if you have read this far, this book might be scaring the crap out of you. That is probably a good thing. If you are brand new and want to really *do* this business and are not just playing around you should plan to *not* do these mistakes and take as long as you need to take with your learning curve.

Do yourself a favor and read this book real slow and think logically about the things it is saying in here. There is no need to be in a hurry and certainly no need to skip over anything because the market is *always* going to be there waiting to pay you. All that is happening in the live markets is a transfer of one traders account to another's. Which trader do you want to be, the trader who is making the same mistakes over and over and paying, or the one who *gets* paid?

I have probably scared you a little bit by now however a little fright can't hurt you at this point, what *can* though is not paying attention to what this book is telling you not to do. Every time you are thinking to yourself "oh I will just come back to that" or "I will just skip that because it is not important" just think about the bon fire at your party or those sharks with the fully loaded revolvers.

What is the best job you never thought of? I bet it wasn't day trader, investor, or high frequency day trader? Was it money manager/day trader, risk manager/day trader? For the type of job I am writing about in this book there isn't even a high school diploma or MBA needed!!! Hell no clothes needed for that matter!

To be a great investor and trader you have to get past the idea that having and making a lot of money are the only ways to happiness. Once you get past that thought process you can and will become successful. You also have to make a decision as to how much time you will put forth into your new trading business.

You absolutely do not need a big fancy degree from a big fancy Ivy League college to become successful at the business of making money with money. All the information you need to do this business is readily available online if you know where to get it. You will need to develop your own time management skills though.

I will talk about where to go to get the information you need to become consistently profitable in this business a little later however right now I want to tell about how good it is to be able to do this business and work for yourself.

First let me say that working from home and making as much money as you could possibly want to have is completely possible. There is no secret about that. Day trading, swing trading and investing are the best business in the world to be in as far as I am concerned.

You can do it from anywhere on the planet there is WIFI so what could be wrong with kicking back on your boat at the marina or at the beach on a beautiful sunny day or flying to Europe to meet friends for the weekend. That's the beautiful thing about the market; you always have a chance to make money. It's virtually 24 hours a day. Just like an ATM right?

I like to think of it as a big ATM machine because it is open virtually 24 hours a day seven days a week just about. You just need to have the proper PIN# to get your money out. Do the training and education and do not make these mistakes in this book and you will be well on your way to having your own personal PIN# to make money in the live markets every day. While the market *is* like a big ATM that is open 24 hours a day if you don't have the *right* PIN# *your money will get sucked into it* of that you can be assured. Learning to trade on demo is not some video game. If you are going to make the decision to learn this business than you had be learn it the right way the first time from the first day.

The amount of time you want to work is up to you. You are the boss right? You make the decisions as to when you want to work and for how long. Since I position trade now I might spend 30 minutes a week analyzing my charts. I suggest if you are brand new to the trading business that you spend at least 10 minutes a day reviewing your positions at the very minimum.

You can pick the best time of day which suits your lifestyle to work in the financial markets. You can work in any session there is in which the markets are open. There are many to choose from so you have the chance to make money when it is convenient for you.

One of the first questions I ask brand new traders who come to me for mentoring is *why* they want to trade. The answer I get *most* of the time is "I want to make money". Hell *we all* want to make money in the market and that should be every investor and traders goal. For me it is to add some money to my account balance monthly as I am a position investor and trader. I look at things on a longer term time horizon.

When I first started out in the business I had not answered any of the serious "*why*" questions and only knew I wanted to make money from trading. I had unrealistic expectations from the start which is only *one* problem most new traders coming into the business have.

Most new people who come into this business have unrealistic expectations on what they will be able to pull out of the market money wise on a daily basis. We have all been there though. Most elite professionals who are at the level of consistency of making money on a daily basis if they are day traders have accepted that the market will only give out so much and they are good with that.

The live markets are an intimidating and brutal place for someone who starts off with the wrong information. They can be a mysterious, murky, and complicated place for the ill advised. By following the advice in this book and keep it simple and taking very slow and absorbing every detail you can have the best chance for a high probability outcome as a successful market participant. Make no mistake the market can make you lose your mind, burn your soul, and help you to lose all your money. Quickly!!

Learning this business is not sexy however it does not have to be mundane and boring either. It is going to take some time. Most consistently profitable investors and traders I know who have made it have in the very high thousands of hours of education, training and screen time.

You can use this book and the references, suggestions and tips in it to go further into your educational studies of the markets and there dynamics. Knowing market dynamics is going to be critical for you to have the winning edge you will need to be a successful market participant. By studying what this book suggests you will not become one of the 97% of the sheeple of the herd.

The live market is not a place for the weak minded or faint hearted. If you have any doubts about your skills or confidence take some advice and just stay out of the live market until you have developed a *kill everyone* mentality because that is what you will need to make real money in there every day.

I had the crazy notion in my mind I was going to make $200 a day from trading my first live account. I look back on that now and think how crazy unrealistic that was. Most brand new traders come into the business under funded as it is anyway and I was no different. You cannot go into the live market on a 5 thousand dollar account and expect to make *anything* however your mind is telling that you can.

If you are brand new and have no knowledge in this business, it is critical that you pay attention to the valuable information that is given in this book if you wish to become successful. There are zero shortcuts to getting there; however, the learning curve does not have to as brutal as most new people make it on themselves.

Almost all brand new investors and traders from all over the world make the mistakes this book talks about. It's almost universal. Once you have read this entire book, I invite you to tell other people you know who are thinking of getting into this business to also buy it and read it, so *you* can help *them*, as well. Help them save time and money, and they will be grateful to you forever.

The information in this book will put you on the *fast track* to learning exactly the information you need to get started making money right away in the live markets. You want to invest and trade, right? You have to learn it the right way from the start to be able to put what you learn in your education to practical use in the live markets and make consistent profits.

When I say *fast track* I don't mean you can just go in the live market after reading this one book. It is imperative then that since you as a retail investor or trader have a look at all the information you need to study even if you are trading intraday which by the way the smart money does not do.

That should be a huge clue, however because people think this is a get rich quick business when they first get into it and they think that they can learn a few chart patterns and some price action and then can go into the live make and make jet fuel money. New traders are buying Ferrari's and Gulfstream 650's before ever making a live trade with real money.

Don't become one of the sheeple of the herd! Ask yourself this question before you begin your education journey for day trading. Do I want to be the one who *pays* in the market *or* do I want to be the one who *gets* paid? Just keep that in mind when you are learning what you need to know about this business and *it is* a business and you should treat it as such.

You are the one who is in control of what you learn, so I encourage you to do the smart thing and do what it takes to become successful. By reading this entire book, you can reach your desired goals in a shorter time if you just don't do what others are doing wrong. Makes sense, right? Learn from others' mistakes and make yourself better. I encourage you to do it, so you will not lose any of your hard-earned money in the markets.

It is very important to have figured out what your ultimate goals are *before* you step foot into the markets with your hard earned real money. Questions I ask new people are: are you trading for short term income or long term wealth building? Are you trying to build up your account balance to be able to take on more risk and trade larger size? I ask them why they want to do this business. I ask them if they know what their goals for the long term are.

If a client cannot answer these questions right away I just encourage them to stay out of the live markets until they can answer them and be honest. I also will ask them how much capital they plan to enter the live markets to work with. There is no point in trying to enter the live markets with scared money.

There are as many different types of market investors and traders as there are assets to invest in. There is no one *good* or *bad* type of investor or trader, and there is no group of investors or traders who will do better than anyone else. Each personality type works in a different way. The markets need *all* types of investors to maintain a healthy balance.

There is a place for all types of investors and traders in the market, and while there are winners and losers in the market, the important thing is to pick a style that works for *you*. Once have you have decided on how you approach the market it is important to stick with your decision.

New people coming into this business make *a lot* of mistakes, one being that they don't know what type of investor or trader they want to be. So when starting out ask yourself. What kind of investor or trader do you desire to be? You should know this *before* beginning this business.

Ask yourself this question. What do you want to be? Are you going to be a stock trader or a futures trader or both? If you are a stock trader have you built a watch list? Do you know how? Do you know how to get data about the companies on your watch list? Do you know how to screen for the best stocks? Do you trade large cap, small cap, or micro-cap?

What kinds of chart do you trade stocks on, daily, monthly, intraday? Are you a day trader, swing trader or market investor of stocks? You should have all of these questions answered *before* studying anything or ever stepping foot in the live market with real money.

I wrote this book as a great introduction to the markets so that brand new investors and traders with zero experience won't have to waste valuable learning time and money to figure out only the most important things to know on their own.

While I do not recommend day trading, it is possible; however, it requires a lot of time, preparation and a very *large* amount risk capital. I know very few successful day traders.

Begin with the end in mind. There are a lot of things to consider when thinking about becoming a professional market investor and trader. Do you like action? Maybe you want to be a scalper and get in and out of trades very quickly and take many trades in one day. You need a speedy internet connection for this type of trading.

If you want to swing trade, you will need to have the capital in your account to handle the overnight margin requirement of whatever your chosen instrument is to work in. CAUTION: If you have to use leverage or margin to trade, you just shouldn't trade especially if you are brand new. Stay out until you have sufficient risk capital to go into the live market and be able to have a chance to make money.

If you would like to be more of an investor or position trader, then you will also need to be well-funded to sustain a draw-down on a position of as much as 50 percent. Should you not have the mental wherewithal to sit through a 50 percent draw-down on any given position in your portfolio, then again I recommend just staying out of the live markets until you have the psychological makeup to do so.

I recommend picking one style of investing or trading and becoming an expert at it. Find a few instruments you like and study their price action and work in those exclusively. You do not need to work in every asset class there is. A big mistake of many beginners is to want to trade everything; you must try to fight that urge.

You must have laser focus, you don't want to be a generalist you want to be a specialist. It is very prudent to try to develop a level of expertise to predict and profit from price fluctuations in every different kind of investment however it is only prudent to do it one at a time.

When you become proficient at the ones you work in exclusively, just add another contract or more shares as your account balance allows. There is no need to learn more information unless you want to switch asset classes completely.

I strongly recommend you know what type of market investor or trader you desire to be and whether you will be active or passive and *before* you start to study or learn any information related to market investing. Being well prepared can help cut down on the long learning curve there is to becoming successful in this business.

It is important to know this information first in order to plan out what type of education and training one will do when entering the learning phase of the knowledge curve. There is a lot to know to be successful in the investing and trading business so it is crucial to know what type of market participant you would like to be in order to not waste any learning time (or hard earned money) for that matter.

The more you can know in advance before *doing anything* or *studying anything* the better you can help yourself to learn only what is needed to get you started in the live market using real money. The rest of what you will need to know can be learned as you go further into the business. I always say start small and build on success.

Learning the right information needed to get started is one of the most critical steps to be a successful market participant over the long term. No one wants to study a lot of information only to find out sometime later that all they needed to know was right there on the chart to begin with.

By the time new traders they realize they have wasted a lot of time and perhaps money on courses and training or books it is very far into their career and business. This only adds to what can be a stressful business as it is anyway. Another thing that happens is that a lot of bad habits can be developed along the way that when brought into a live market situation can be problematic and cause an investor or trader to begin to lose money right away. No one wants that.

Have you studied money management?

I always suggest learning risk management and money management first when mentoring new investors and traders coming into the business that come to me for help. It is the one thing that in the course of my own education and training spent a little time on however not enough. It is one the thing that can save you from having a catastrophic outcome in the business.

Experienced successful investors and traders know that employing a rule based money management strategy is one of critical concepts of risk management. Money management for account preservation is not sexy at all and very boring to study however they are the most important skills in investing and trading that person in the business need to have an understanding of and to have mastered.

If you cannot fully grasp and understand the implications of money management as well as how to actually implement money management principles and techniques, you have a very limited chance of becoming a consistently profitable trader. Until you completely understand and are comfortable with how to have, and how to follow a money management plan I encourage you to stay out of the live market.

Being decisive to smooth your equity curve and managing risk effectively are the skills which should be focused on learning first versus last and unfortunately most losing retail investors and traders don't realize this until it is too late. This is what makes consistently profitable investors and traders different than unprofitable investors and traders.

Not learning proper trade and money management – Not using stop losses and cutting losses early. You hear that a million times in your investing and trading career. Why is it then that almost every brand new investor and trader lacks this skill? They have not taken the time to learn this very important skill from the start and it almost always causes them some account pain in the beginning.

The very *first* thing that a brand new trader should learn and understand completely is risk and money management. To many times I have had people come to me for mentoring help and I ask them how much time they spent on learning money management and they say "what do you mean"?

Money management in the live market is what it is all about not trading. You don't actually make money by trading you make money by being in the market *in* your position. If you don't have any money left you can't *be* in the market.

Learning money management requires time and attention to detail that most all new traders are not willing to do. Once you have a live position in the market you go from be a trader to a risk and money manager. The only thing you have control over once you are in the live market is how much money you *don't lose*.

To succeed at trading the financial markets, you need to not only thoroughly understand position sizing, and risk amount per trade, you also need to consistently execute each of these aspects of money management in combination with a highly effective yet simple to understand trading strategy that uses price action in conjunction with supply and demand principles.

To be consistently profitable over the long term one must consider capital preservation their number one rule. To be successful in this business it cannot be any other way. It takes money to make money in the market and <u>once it is *gone it is gone*</u>. This is why I tell clients they must study risk and money management *first and foremost*.

Trading is a risk taking business and if you are not properly prepared to take on a certain amount of risk to gain a reward then perhaps investing and trading is not for you. Remember it takes money to make money and if you go into the live market without the proper training and without a rule based plan with very strict money management you will be out of the game before you are in it. Having the psychological make up to employ money management is what makes the successful investor and trader successful.

Do you know what makes you tick?

You must be true to yourself from the start in this business. Only when an investor or trader has experienced hard losses or even blown out their account do they start to work on their psychology for investing and trading. They have ignored the subject from the start of their education and training and not bothered to look inside themselves.

Unfortunately they wait too long and try to un-do the bad habits which have already been developed. This is very hard to do and sometimes too little too late. This is why I put this psychology part second in the first things a brand new trader needs to know. It is a very important aspect of the learning process which needs to take place *before* going in the live markets with real money.

You must build a rock solid foundation of principles to work from in investing and trading and the psychological base is no different than the trading base. You must have it from the beginning to become successful. You must develop structure and discipline that is unbending. Brand new traders just jump right in thinking they "got it" however most of the time they don't.

Having structure and discipline are traits of the most successful investors and traders. Having these two traits among others are critical to being a professional self-directed Forex trader. Without them it will be very hard to become consistently profitable on a daily basis.

When clients come to me for mentoring one of the first things I ask them is if they have looked inside themselves. The only place a trader becomes successful from is within. A mentor or a trading coach can only help a new investor or trader so much. New aspiring traders must look within themselves and figure out what they need to do to enhance and perfect their performance in the live market.

As a brand new beginner it is imperative that you have your self under control *before* you ever step foot in the live market and execute a position with your hard earned real money. Trading psychology in Forex futures and stock trading is very important and is something that new traders do not understand.

There are many things involved in trading that can cause emotional swings that can affect your trading decisions. Lack of self-control in the markets leads to stress, anxiety and ultimately money loss. No one wants that however most new traders coming into the business are looking for instant gratification and quick money. This leads to a lot of *very bad* decisions and self-sabotage in new traders and it can get *verrrrry* ugly!

I tell all new investors and traders they *must* have their emotions under control *before* they ever set foot in the live markets and put their hard earned money to work. It is one thing to learn how to execute your trading plan on a demo account to learn how the platform you will be utilizing to execute your positions in the live market. It is entirely another thing to do it flawlessly in a live market environment using real money with the best market participants in the world.

Once you have your psychology and emotions under control you will achieve consistency and be able to make as much money in the live markets as you desire. Combine that with solid money management principles and you will have become a professional investor and trader.

Have you composed a good journal to help you with analysis?

One thing all investors and traders I personally know do is that they all have kept a trading journal of their activities in the live market. This journal acts as an analysis tool when determining what is working and what did not work. I know of no successful person in this business that has not done this.

These traders are very diligent about putting every piece of information about their trading activities into their journal. Some are more comprehensive than others. It all depends on what type of investing and trading you are doing however the more information you can have at your disposal the better analysis you will be able to perform.

The amount of analysis that can be done in a journal to better develop an edge in the live markets can be unlimited depending on the amount of detail that is incorporated into the journal design. Doing analysis on journal data can be of the utmost importance to an investor and trader to determine what mistakes if any are being made and repeated.

It sometimes takes a brand new trader 3-5 years to learn this business. By doing what it says in this book you can cut your time down to 30 days or even less depending on how fast you can grasp the principles presented here. Using a daily chart requires you to look at less information on a daily basis.

It is up to you to do the work and get the practice time in. I encourage you to journal your trades from day one so you can see how you progress, where you made mistakes, and how you improved and built up your account size.

While it may seem like a lot of work to document every trade you take in a journal, it needs to be done. You should get into the habit of doing it every day you work in the market, right from the beginning of your trading business and career. At the end of the day, you should annotate every chart and then print it out, or create a document on your computer and store it there.

This journal will help you to become a better investor and trader over time and will act as a reference of what you did that worked and what you did that did not work. It will also give you an edge over those traders who do not do it and are trying to wing it.

There is no substitute for being prepared, and a journal can certainly help you to prepare for your workday by reviewing the previous day's price action. You can also build your trading plan for the current day from this data, as well.

If you want to be successful in the markets and have an edge over others, this is one of the ways to do it. A journal is a useful tool and gives you the highest probability of having a successful outcome at your investing and trading business, although it is just one of many. As a new investor and trader it is a must-have item.

You should learn to journal your market activity both on demo and in the live market. There are plenty of journal templates on line that you can download and use as a baseline for your own, and then once you are prepared the right way you can add or delete information from your journal as needed.

If you find that you are still taking too many losses, you can refer to your journal and then you can move back to the simulator and remedy the problem, and then go back in the live market and try it again. It took me two tries of going in the live market with real money and losing some of it before I was ready. I was smart enough to know I was not prepared enough and got out before I blew out. Look in your journal and analyze what you have done previously that worked and did not.

It is recommended that you always give yourself enough time to try all the different markets before picking one that best suits you. What market best fits your personality as a trader? In which market do you see the best price action? Have these questions answered before thinking about using real money in the live markets.

If you journal your market activity, you will be able to go back over time and see what positions worked the best. There are going to be losses. It's part of doing this business, and if you try to win all the time, you will lose more. It is not realistic to think you can win 90 percent of your positions.

Sounds crazy, but ask successful real money traders and that's what they will tell you. If you take a loss, journal it, analyze it, learn from it, and move on. The next thousand trades are waiting for you in the market. That's the beautiful thing about this business. The market is always going to be there waiting to pay you. Are you prepared to get paid?

You can start a journal at the forum where you are learning and also on your own. It can be a Word file, Excel file or just a plain Notepad file. You can also take screenshots of all your charts and save them to a picture file. Many traders post screenshots of their charts in the forums.

You must be able rationalize why you did things the way you did them when in the live market. You are in control of all the variables that enable you to have a positive outcome as a market participant. So have some control and even journal why you did it a certain way.

No one is making you do this business but you. I sound like a broken record however if *you* don't take action for what *you* do in the live market and you run with the sheeple of the herd *you* are the one who will be broke. Trust me on that!

A competitive edge includes as I said earlier a mental edge with discipline, laser focus, and a fail-proof strategy. Enforcing some psychological rules in your strategy is critical and following them at all costs will absolutely make sure you can beat the competition. I always say that if you are a known rule breaker, then just don't establish too many. However, the ones you *do* have must be followed as if your very life depended on them. Journaling can help give you the edge you need to be a successful market participant for the long term.

Did you compose a rules based plan for your style of trading?

In live market trading it helps to keep the decision making process as consistent and objective as possible. Using a rules based plan for your trading is a *must* and is a trait all successful investors and traders I know possess. A winning plan should be able to sustain your profitability over time in order that you can *keep* all your hard earned profits you make from the markets.

The reality of it is that too many undisciplined new traders don't spend enough time composing a rules based plan for the type of trading they wish to do. I have my clients think about what their monetary goals are and then help them compose a great trading plan, becoming a great trader, and attaining their goals.

There is no room for excuses in the professional traders mind and thus they know that they are the final decision maker on what is being done or *NOT* done. They are in complete control of all aspects of their trading plan. They have mastered keeping their emotions fully controlled and are aware they are in control of the destiny of there long term investment strategy and management of their portfolio. This is one of the things that make them so successful and it is *all done by following their rule based plan*.

I tell *all* new people I help out that what you will find is that over the course of your learning curve and time in the live markets that you will ultimately find that what is going to work for you and make you money every day or month is a combination of things you have learned over time and have put together to make *your own* winning rule based plan. What works for one trader *will not* work the same way for another however that does not mean you cannot adapt different ideas to fit your own trading style.

Developing a trading plan takes a lot of hard work sometimes as much if not more than actually learning how to trade and operate your platform. It takes time to see what works for you and what does not. It also takes a lot of time to develop the rules that go along with your trading plan. Having a plan and some rules are critical in this business. To not have them and stick to them is a recipe for financial disaster and account ruin.

All traders who have become consistently profitable use a solid uncomplicated rule based plan. They have achieved their long term success by properly executing their plan flawlessly over and over and over again. They are prepared at all times and this is just one of the traits that make them successful.

It doesn't matter how many or how few rules you have in your plan. Most investors and traders I know who are consistently profitable on a daily basis have a simple plan that is perhaps one page or less. It is one thing to have a plan it is however the most important thing to do is to *follow the plan at all costs*. I always say if you are a known rule breaker then just don't too many however you must have *some*.

One exercise I like my clients to do to get them in the habit of following their plan is to pretend they are an airline pilot and they have to follow a checklist at all times and never break any procedural rules or all lives could be lost. Airline pilots by the way are some of the best investors and traders out there in the business today. They are used to doing what I just described and will not deviate for any reason.

Take the last paragraph and just imagine that your account balance is the lives and if you do not follow your plan *all* of your money could be lost. Make no mistake you can perhaps lose *all* of your money by not having and following a plan.

Successful investors and traders know that that having a simple plan is the only way to have a profitable significant edge in the live markets. A plan does not have to be complicated to be successful and these consistently profitable investors and traders have come to realize this and actually use the simplest methods in investing and trading which is supply and demand.

One of the things that traders do is they get monitoring their positions confused with trade management. If you have followed your rules based plan and determined your entry and exit as well as your stop loss and profit target there should be nothing to do really.

What I mean by monitoring your position is to make sure your automated strategy if you are using one is doing what it is supposed to be doing. This is critical as even the best automated strategy can have a discombobulation at some point.

A well-known Forex educator said in one of his webinars I listened to some time ago that he is a big advocate of always monitoring positions. He had been using an automated robot to assist in putting on positions. His robot started to put on positions and malfunctioned. What happened to him was he lost 30% of his live account working capital in 24 hours because he was not monitoring what was happening.

I only recommend using an automated system if you are using it for putting on and taking off positions as well as executing a stop loss and profit target at the same time as the position is being executed in the live market. Then it is truly hands off. All you need to do at that point is to **keep your hands off** the mouse and let the market do all the heavy lifting for you. *Can* you do that?

Until you can monitor your live market positions without actually doing *anything* I strongly recommend that you stay out of the real live market with your hard earned real money. Just because you are monitoring what is going on *does not* mean you have to take any action!

The sooner you can get your head around that last statement the more money you will be able to make. That's is what you are in this business for so have some control and do what needs to be done to become successful. Be disciplined and don't make the mistakes this book details. Do not become one of the sheeple of the herd and do what everyone else does and study what everyone else studies.

Learn to think independently and make money for yourself for the rest of your life!

Use supply and demand for advanced trading selection

The absolute biggest advantage professionals have when it comes to being successful in investing and trading is having stuck with it. That's when you can feel good and know that no one did it but you. The more you try to find the Holy Grail and jump from method to method the less chance you will have to succeed in trading hence the 97% failure rate. Those of us who *have* made it and *are* successful have traveled a looooong road.

As I said previously in this book if you are not willing to put in the time to learn this business the right way from the start and do the proper education and training it might be best for you to think about another profession.

This next section is going to give you some basic information about supply and demand and how to do advanced trading and investing with it in the live markets in real time with real money.

The core of what is presented in this book is how *ALL* markets work which is on the principle of supply and demand. There is no mention of anything other than what needs to be learned from the start of your trading/investing career. It is learning supply and demand investing and trading and price action. That's what you need to focus on from the start if you want to be successful right away. That is what works in today's financial markets for making money. You want to make money right?

This book is going to be your starting point to learn advanced trading and investing the right way the first time so as not to develop any bad habits that can cost you money in the live markets. Learning this information in this way will cut down your learning curve will enable you to get on the *fast track* to making real money as well as giving you the edge you need to have from the time you begin your new business instead of spending a lot of time learning information that is not going to help you and is not realistic in the live markets.

TIP Don't waste your time or your hard earned money on learning things that won't help you in live markets and perhaps could cause you to lose money. Only do what you know to be true.

You do not need to over think *anything* in supply and demand (S&D) trading. It is very simple, the simplest in fact. I had to unlearn 95% of what I had already studied before I became consistently profitable on a daily basis in the markets. My goal is to save you brand new traders and investors who are new and wanting to learn trading a lot of time and cut down your learning curve so you can be on your way to making real money in the live markets every day. How fast you "get it" is up to you.

OK traders the next place you need to go and the next thing you need to start to grasp is basics and foundation then application of these supply and demand principles in the live markets. You can do a search online for a supply and demand foundation and application courses. I encourage you to watch every video and read every article and book you can on this style of investing and trading.

Here is a good start for you brand new investors and traders looking to understand supply and demand dynamics and use it to invest and trade in the live markets of today. It is economics 101 pretty much. You should learn it though if you want to know and understand what really makes price do what it does in the live market because it is this and nothing else.

So that I do not sound redundant in my explanations after we move on from this point I will direct you to go here: http://www.investopedia.com/university/economics/economics3. asp for an explanation of the dynamics of supply and demand which will from this point be the only thing mentioned as far as a way of investing and trading is concerned in the live market.

Supply and demand is not rocket science and no one owns it, or has a patent on it and anyone can learn it. It is a simple market principle that has been in existence since there was a market. It will always be the same principle till there is no more market which will be the end of days.

You do not have to be a math wizard to get it and you do not have to memorize any formulas or math equations. It is just a simple yet powerful principle that when armed with its knowledge and the knowledge of the price action of your chosen instrument of choice you can have a serious winning edge which will give you the highest probability of having a positive outcome on being a market participant.

It all builds off of this basic principle of supply and demand right here so I encourage you to take your time and absorb it a little at a time. You will see that it is a robust and repeatable process in *any* market and *any* time frame. It does not matter if you are trading equities, Forex futures, grains or kittens and puppies for that matter. You just have to pick what TF (time frame) you like and what market(s) you want to invest in or trade and what your comfort level of risk is in those markets. As I said it is fairly simple once you have it down pat.

A lot of trading books teach a top down or a bottom up approach how about the right way approach and doing it the right way from day one. Mostly all of the trading books teach this business not only wrong but they teach it unrealistically. Why would you want to learn this way?

If you are thinking that trading and investing in the live market with your hard earned real money is going to be easy and you are going to make millions of dollars doing it you are in for a rude and very expensive awakening. Don't get me wrong you *can* and *will* some make money every day in the live markets perhaps *LOTS OF*

IT if you do what it says in this book. Nothing in the market is guaranteed. It's about putting all the probabilities of having a positive outcome in your favor.

Learn to see unfilled orders on a price chart and the PA of your preferred instrument to trade and you are home. No fancy news, no indicators just PA and what makes the market do what it does, supply and demand. It's *THE* only thing that makes the market move. Simple really however traders tend to make things hard on themselves and cause a lot account pain because of it. Don't be *that* investor or trader. People just think this is a get rich quick business. It's precisely the opposite unless you are a Wall Street bank or hedge fund.

As I said this is not a get rich quick business. You can become well off, have financial security and freedom to do anything you want in this business. You can do it anywhere in the world. It takes time and patience though and it involves a lot of waiting around till the market comes to you and gives you what you want. Yes that's right you can actually make the market do exactly what you want and I will tell you how.

Having spent a lot of time on studying and learning trading, reading charts and indicators when all I needed to look at was right there on the chart in front of my eyes all the time every day all day, price action. It does not lie, it cannot. It does precisely the opposite it tells you where the supply and demand in the market is and thus where to make your move. If you are using a daily chart you don't need to look at too much information.

I spent days, night's weekend's holidays on studying the aspects of trading that I thought, and that all the educational books tell you will make a better trader. I can't disagree more now with most of that information. Was learning it a waste of time? No absolutely not!

The road I took was an enlightening one and I learned a great amount about how geo-economics and geo-politics work and how the world really runs and works. *SO* no it was not a waste of my time at all. I love to learn and in the course of my education in trading and investing have become an expert at finding data.

A price chart is the graphical representation of how a financial instrument travels to supply and demand value areas over a set period of time. The chart shows where price action is and also where it *is not*. In other words how long did price spend in a value area and how far away from the area did it travel over time before returning to that value area.

Why price moves in these ways is to get to the areas we will be discussing shortly. It is only based on one thing and that is supply and demand in the market. Learning to be able to visually spot this on a price chart is most important for you to be able to make real money in the live markets every day.

You can go online and start to look at price charts and you will see how price action works in the live markets. Look up some charting courses. You do not need to pay for anything as there is a vast amount of *free* information on charting online. You *can* and *should* get a demo account and begin to study the charting tools in your chosen platform.

http://www.informedtrades.com/index.php has a huge amount of free courses for the brand new investor and trader. Simit the owner over there has done a fine job at compiling all the data and information that a brand new investor and trader will need to know and can study there for free. You can journal there and also get mentoring from real money investors and traders to help you expedite your learning curve.

Other than knowing that PA only goes up, down and sideways and using candle sticks to see this PA on the price charts it is very basic and really all you need to know. Traders and investors often make it very hard on themselves by trying to digest too much information (TMI). This only leads to losing money and is not recommended.

The human brain can only process so much information at one time. If you keep it simple than that's what it will be, don't over think it. I strongly encourage you to keep this fact as part of your trading and investing plan as it will serve you well for the rest of your career in your investing and trading business.

The other main thing you need to be able to read on the price chart is where the unfilled orders of the smart money reside in the live market. You need to be able to see this at a glance then quantify it and use the information to make a decision whether you would like to enter the market where the smart money are entering the market and be a participant along with them.

There are many types of ways that traders use to see this price action however the only true real thing is the price action itself. There will not be any discussion of any other method of use other than supply and demand as well as price action in this book. All of the trading principles used in this book and methods presented are simple supply and demand because that is the only thing that moves the markets. The only thing!

What you need to know now is how price action on a chart works and what supply and demand are and how they are the only things that move price from one value area of the chart to another.

That's the beauty of it this method. It works on *all* liquid markets and on *any time frame* you choose to look at it on. I encourage you to work on daily charts because that is what the smart money uses. Once you can see the value areas on the daily chart you can see them on any time frame. That's what makes this method so lethal. It's the combination of price action and supply and demand value areas. That is what wins in today's markets.

Here are some tips for using supply and demand to trade stocks (or any other asset class). Look for the way PA leaves a value area on the chart. Also look at how much time PA actually spent in a value area. These are two critical pieces of information. Another thing to look for is how far PA moved away from the value area before returning to it.

This information gives you your profit margin and price target information. Look up a foundation course that teaches you this valuable information. They are available online for free. Do a search for supply and demand foundation and application and study it hard if you want to be a winner in today's tough markets.

Your rule based plan should include your criteria for entry and exit using supply and demand value area information. This information should also have your risk reward criteria as well. If you're set up does not give you the correct risk reward that fits your plan criteria then it is up to you to make the decision to not take action. To do so would not be following your plan.

In supply and demand trading it is all about putting the probabilities in your favor. All you should be looking for are low risk high reward high probability entries on the chart you are working on. If it's not there *IT'S NOT THERE*!

I encourage you to study and use supply and demand trading. You can find a great supply and demand learning thread here: http://www.forexfactory.com/showthread.php?t=428204 Alfonso over there does an awesome job and goes above and beyond what any trader should do to teach brand new traders supply and demand trading. You should buy him a Ferrari when you become successful. Don't worry that it is a Forex related thread; supply and demand trading works on *any* liquid asset class on *any* time frame you chose to look at and trade from.

Go there and learn with the other new traders who are there. All the rules of using supply and demand for trading are listed on the first page of the forum. There *plenty* of chart examples as well. You can also do a search online for a foundation and application course for supply and demand. They are online for *free* for anyone who can find the information.

The road to success in the business of investing and trading is paved with the wreckage of blown accounts of novice retail traders who did not take the time to do the education, the practice, and the psychological development necessary to become consistently profitable in this business. Don't be *that* trader!

Don't become one of the sheeple of the herd and do what everyone else is doing when and where they are doing it. The smart money can see this on the chart and are looking to take advantage of the errors the sheeple of the herd make over and over again.

Picking a method or having a system that works in the market is critical to your success as a market participant. The one thing new people in the business do that causes them problems is that they get going on something they found, or have heard about, or purchased, and then not stay with it. It takes time for something to work, although nothing works forever. However, if you cannot give it a chance to succeed for you, then you are selling yourself short (no pun intended).

This is a big mistake new people make in the business. The minute they have a couple of losses in the live market and lose some of their money, they think that the method or system that caused them to lose is no good. They jump from method to method and never settle on anything for a given period of time and allow it to work for them. In the meantime, they continue to lose money. They are always seeking the Holy Grail method, and while it *does* exist, it is not what you think.

I recommend learning a method of investing and trading that can be used over all asset classes and on any time frame. The only method I found that does this and works in the live market, because that is what the live markets work on, is *supply and demand*. I combined that with the price action of the instruments I work in, and it has become a lethal money making combination.

I think what you will find over time is that what works is a combination of things you have learned during your time in the business. It doesn't matter *what* they are as long as they work for *you* and are making *you* money. *That* is honestly the Holy Grail in investing and trading, *PERIOD*.

I recommend picking one style of investing or trading such as supply and demand and becoming an expert at it. Find a few instruments you like and study their price action and work in those exclusively. You *do not* need to work in every asset class there is. When you become proficient at the ones you work in exclusively, just add another contract as your account balance allows. There is no need to learn more information unless you want to switch asset classes completely.

A friend of mine who introduced me to the business said something to me once that hit me like he had punched me in the face. He said, "Why would you want to learn a bunch of different things instead of knowing a few things that consistently make you money every day?" My advice to the new investors and traders I mentor now is to learn the price action of one to three instruments intimately, and then once they are familiar with them and become consistently profitable working in those instruments, they begin adding more contracts.

My goal with this section of this book is to save you brand new traders and investors who are and wanting to learn investing and trading a lot of time and cut down your learning curve so you can be on your way to making real money in the live markets every day. How fast you "*get it*" is up to you. If you pay close attention to the mistake examples in this book and not make them you can greatly increase your learning curve time.

The amount of time it can take to become consistently profitable on a daily basis with real money in the live markets can be lengthy. Some traders and investors I know including myself have in the very high thousands of hours of looking at and analyzing charts. The amount of screen time needed to be able to go in the live market and make real money is said to be 10,000 or more hours. Hopefully this book will help get you started and cut down that amount of learning curve time.

I do not listen to news, I do not use any indicators, and there is no fancy system or method. You don't even have to learn any equations or mathematics, its simple price action, supply and demand, along with training your eyes to see where unfilled smart money orders reside at in the live market. *THAT* is where you want to be and *THAT* is where you want to trade from and *THAT* is who you want to be looking for to trade along with. It gives you the highest probability of having a positive outcome of making money in the live markets.

How to set it and forget it for high profits – patience pays handsomely

Set it and forget it trading is also one of the names for supply and demand trading. In this type of method you set your resting order in the market based on your rules and analysis and then just wait for price action to come to you. Investing and trading is a business that is all about patience. It is a lot of waiting around for a price to get to where you need it to be to make your money. That can take a while sometimes. It requires an iron will not to chase the price or to see something that is just not there. Doing these last two, chasing and seeing things that are not there, will get a new trader into a lot of trouble.

The waiting is the hardest part. That is a line in a Tom Petty song. It is the truest thing there could be in trading as far as I am concerned. Most people coming into this business are a bit misguided thinking they can beat the market. I won't say no one beats the market however it is very few who actually do. It is mostly hedge funds who are using OPM (other people's money) and a lot of leverage which is most of the time money they borrowed from the Wall Street bankers or is it bankster's? Hmmmmm.

In S&D it's all about setting your position order and then just waiting and letting PA come to you. It's just a waiting game at that point. If you get filled there then you are in the market with everything already there. *IF* you do not get filled then you just cancel the order and reassess PA and look for the next signal and opportunity. Traders tend to want to see things that don't exist and it gets them into trouble.

Successful investors and traders know that that having a simple plan is the only way to have a profitable significant edge in the live markets. A plan does not have to be complicated to be successful and these consistently profitable investors and traders have come to realize this and actually use the simplest methods in investing and trading which is supply and demand.

After having read this entire book you will hopefully know how to have the self-control and patience to wait until price gets to where *you* need it to be to enter the market with confidence. Patience means points! It can take a while to develop this part of the mindset and mentality needed to be a consistently profitable investor and trader. I know it did for me. Once I had my 'AHH ha!' moment, there was no looking back.

As has been said many times before investing and trading is not a get rich quick business. It is precisely the opposite. It is a waiting around for the market to pay you type of business. If you can learn to have patience and be decisive and always follow your trading plan at all costs you can make a handsome living investing and trading the markets. If you trade Forex just repeat this mantra to yourself: patience means pips and for futures patience means points.

You can certainly get the kind of steady, compounding return that investment pros seek and you can do it yourself at minimal cost and risk. All it takes is a broader view of the opportunities in the markets and the *patience* to see a serious investing or retirement plan through to the end.

When it all started to come together for me it was not until I start using the principles of supply and demand in conjunction with price action that I started to really see a change in my profits. I had to go back and learn the basics of what supply and demand are to be able to understand how to utilize them in the live market. Supply and demand is the only thing that moves price in the market.

Now I can place a resting order in the live market, get driven to the airport, board a plane a fly anywhere on the planet with confidence and zero fear. I truly set and forget. Stops are in emotion is out as it were.

When you work according to your plan there is no room for greed because everything you are doing is already *predetermined*. I do not like to have my money exposed in the live market any longer than is necessary to have a positive outcome. I now run my own Nano hedge fund and have multiple open positions in the live market at one time at any given moment.

The thing I count on knowing is that my stop loss and profit targets are in the live market as well. There is nothing but time at this point which has enabled me to write this book you are reading and all the others I have out currently. When you do a set it and forget it trade you had better have done your homework!

I am also a firm believer that knowledge is power and that the more you know about the assets you are working in the better. Having a research and education plan as part of your operating plan for the market is one more way you can push back fear. The more educated you are about what you are doing the less fear you are likely to have when working in the live markets with real money. This will also let you have the confidence in your skills to truly set and forget trade for high profits. Remember the less time you have to think about what you need to do and the less time you have your hand on the mouse the better off and more profitable you will be.

Consistently profitable investors and traders will identify and remove any and *all* barriers that can be psychologically keeping them from having a positive outcome in the markets. I like to do this by quantifying price action on the chart and then setting and forgetting my trade with true confidence. What will you do?

Use probability boosters for low risk high reward trade selection

Your job now as a professional investor and trader is to manage your money and control risk at *all* costs. You are basing all of the decisions you make on your developed logic—not with emotions. You are confident that you would much rather pursue a low risk entry than a small loss if it should happen. It is only low risk, high reward and high probability outcomes that you are looking for now, just like the Wall Street banks and the smart money.

There are some things called probability boosters that can help you determine the validity of these areas and also help you to quantify them as well. I will be discussing those probability boosters shortly.

Professionals are able to know what the 'sheeple of the herd' are doing even before they do it because they can read a price chart and know where the supply and demand value areas are and where the smart money has their resting orders in the live market. Then they just enter where those orders are and sit back and make money off the smart money's volume.

All professional investors and traders I know are prepared *before* they step foot in the live markets and know there is no such thing as winning every single time. It's just not realistic. They know before they enter a position what their odds are of having a positive outcome. They have stacked probability in their favor and have the confidence to be in there competing against the best investors and traders on the planet. They do this with probability boosters.

Along with chart reading goes with looking to only enter at low risk high reward high probability value areas. These supply and demand value areas are where price action makes its turns in the live markets. Price turns there because that is where the unfilled orders of the smart money reside at in the live market. Probability boosters can help you to see these orders.

Once you have trained your eyes to see where these value areas are on a price chart where the unfilled orders are you will have an edge that the 97% of the sheeple of the herd do not have and you can start making money from the mistakes they make. These supply and demand value areas are easy to spot once you know *what* you are looking for and *where* to look for it on the chart.

Experienced investors and traders know when to enter. They don't chase the market and let price come to them to give them what they need and let the market do *all* of the dirty work for them. They are successful because they know they don't have to take every set up and that they can afford to miss out on something that would have perhaps had a positive outcome for them and they know that there will be plenty more opportunities coming right up.

They only are looking for set ups which offer a low risk high reward outcome that have the highest probability of success for them and is the only thing that matters to them. Professionals only execute a position that that has a stop loss which is as close to their entry as possible to have the lowest amount of risk on the position and consider this a most critical part of their risk management plan.

They are aware of how they will do this even *before* they execute a trade. They also know what their profit margin is as well as their margin of error before taking a position also. The probability boosters they use in their rule based plan give an extra edge.

Once you know what the picture of imbalance is and how to see it on a price chart you can then begin to make money alongside the smart money and professional traders who know what they are looking at. What does it look like on a price chart? You can see many examples of this at the supply and demand learning thread link I provided for you earlier in this book.

What you are looking for is the way price action leaves an area and what fashion it leaves the area from. Did it move away fast, slow, medium speed? How far out did price action go before coming back to the area it left from?

What you are going to see in these areas of imbalance is that price had very little trading going on there and very little volume as well. If you think about how you may have heard price works in a conventional way it is that there is a lot of price action at this area and there is a lot of volume there.

The most important thing you need to remember in learning supply and demand trading is that price on a chart shows you what has *already* happened and where it happened from. What is important to you is not where price traded at but where price *could not* trade at. When price was trading at this value area it could not stay there for any period of time, why? Once you can see this picture of imbalance of price you can begin to quantify and make trading decisions from the information you get from your price charts.

The smart money leaves huge tracks in the market when they move price with their power and money. They can't hide this footprint they leave and it is your job to track them and then do what they are doing where they are doing it from. The probability boosters help you track the smart money's movements and then take advantage of the way they move price to the next value area.

While there are quite a few of the probability boosters you can study and utilize in your trading and investing. I will give you the four main ones now in this book then you can go out and do a search online for the rest of them and then pick which ones you may want to use and incorporate into the rule based plan you will be using to trade with.

The four biggest probability boosters are: How much time did price spend at a value area? How fast did price move away from the value area? How far did price move away from the value area before returning to it? Has price action ever been back to that area yet?

Next is some *basic* information on what to look for and how to use the information you get from the probability boosters to enhance your having a positive outcome as a live market participant.

How much time did price spend at a value area? The less time spends at a level, the more out of balance supply and demand is at the level. Most significant and key turns in price will happen here, and there will be very few candles and/or little volume. The more out of balance supply and demand is the less trading activity there will be at the level. The less time PA spends at the level the more out of balance S&D is at the level, look for 3-8 candles this is the most ideal and volume will be low here.

What you are looking for is the *way* PA leaves the certain area which is said to be a supply or demand value area. This value area is also sometimes called a base or PA can be said to be basing. It is critical that you train your eyes to recognize these areas to acquire your positions from. This is where price is in balance for the moment. The way PA leaves this value area is a key piece of data for you to use in your analysis of any position you may be thinking of taking in the live market with real money. PA will normally leave a value area when it is out of balance with a huge move in PA.

How fast did price move away from the value area? What you are looking for is the way PA leaves the certain area which is said to be a supply or demand value area. How did it move away from the area, was it gradually or an explosive gap? Gap is best and indicates huge imbalance. Explosive is next best and then gradually. Price will come back to the area in same manner it left normally. The stronger the move away from a level the more out of balance S&D is at the level. When the last order is filled at the value area and there are no more buyers or sellers, price must leave the area.

This huge move is normally seen as a large expanded range candle (ERC) or a bunch of them. Does not matter what color you make your candles and I suggest you just have them the same color as the color of the candles will make no difference as to what data the candle is telling you. The *only* people that can make an ERC in the live market are the smart money.

All that matters is that you understand and become an expert at what to see, quantify it and where it is happening. When PA comes back and revisits this value area again in the future is when you want to be there waiting with your resting order in the live market. Here is another tip. You already can see where price traded at. You need to see and quantify where price *could not* trade at.

How far did price move away from the value area before returning to it? The farther price moves away from a level before returning the greater the profit margin and higher the probability of a successful trade. You should only execute a position in the markets only after having determined your profit margin and risk.

You should know *exactly* what your profit target and stop loss will be *before* entry. You can determine this by knowing where the supply and demand areas are on the chart you plan to work on. How far did prices rally up from demand level or down from a supply level before coming back to it. That is the initial profit margin.

Your rules should tell you what you are looking for. If you are looking to get 2:1 then the move away from the area should have been 2 times the measurement of the value area or better. This is how you determine your initial profit margin. It will be up to *you* to decide how much money you are looking to make on any given position. Being conservative can make you a nice living.

Has price action ever been back to that area yet? The more original the area is, the higher probability that price will return to that area. Why is that? Because there are more unfilled orders left there which were not executed from when PA was there previously. The first time PA comes back to this original value area is the best and highest probability chance of having a positive outcome on a position. How far does PA go back into the value area once it returns for the first time? The further it goes in the more orders are used up at that level. Here is a great tip. Once PA goes 25% into the value area stop taking it.

After the first time PA comes back to the value area your odds of having a positive outcome start becoming diminished. There is no need to execute another position from this area again if you have already had a positive outcome and made some money. Don't get greedy!

Here are some tips for using supply and demand to trade stocks (or any other asset class). Look for the way PA leaves a value area on the chart. Also look at how much time PA actually spent in a value area. These are two critical pieces of information. Another thing to look for is how far PA moved away from the value area before returning to it. This information gives you your profit margin and price target information.

Your rule based plan should include your criteria for entry and exit using supply and demand value area information. This information should also have your risk reward criteria as well. If you're set up does not give you the correct risk reward that fits your plan criteria then it is up to you to make the decision to not take action. To do so would not be following your plan.

In supply and demand trading it is all about putting the probabilities in your favor. All you should be looking for are low risk high reward high probability entries on the chart you are working on. If it's not there *IT'S NOT THERE*! Another way to enhance the information you can get from supply and demand value areas on the price chart you are working is to use multiple time frame analysis (MTF). I will have another book coming out on MTF soon so be watching for it.

Successful traders make sure they have a solid foundation in the basics of trading. I know of no successful trader that doesn't have a very good understanding of supply and demand value areas and doesn't know the price action of the chart(s) for the assets they work in.

I'll just say here that supply and demand is the only thing that moves price in the live market and you should study how to use it in your trading if you would like to be successful and make consistent high profits on daily basis.

The most highly successful investors and traders I know and have studied have done what it takes from the very beginning of their time in the business to attain a high level of consistency. They know that is about having all the right information to be able to make the type of high level decisions needed to make money in the live markets.

Automate for truly hands off trading

The consistently profitable investor and trader only enters a position based on their plan which normally calls for the stop loss and profit target to be already known before the position is even entered. I personally use an automated entry so there is no emotion in it. I just set the entry parameter in the live market and when I am filled everything is done for me. All I need do at that point is wait to get paid. There is zero stress, zero drama, and zero complications.

There is no letting a position that is in profit come back to turn into a loser due to having the stop loss already in the live market. I have entered the position *already knowing* what my stop loss amount is money wise so there is no question as to how much I will lose should the position not work out as planned. Once the profit target is hit the position automatically closes and then it is time to look for the next opportunity.

Most professionals have what I call "smart plans" meaning their position is managed from the time it is executed in the live market until the time it closes itself out at the designated profit target. Notice I said closes *itself* out. That is because most professionals including me use an automated system to do their trading.

My system executes my trade and places the stop loss and profit target right when the trade is executed. There is no doing anything manually. Once the position is executed it either makes money or gives me a small but manageable loss. Most of the time, I don't even look at the chart while the trade is working.

The best way to filter out fear and greed from your trading is to automate it. When you see your criteria of your rule based plan is set up in the market you should set your resting order in the live market and then your automated plan do all the work for you. The chart tells you what to do and where to do it you just have to have a solid plan for what to do with the information the chart gives you.

If you don't really see an S&D level then hey guess what *don't enter*!! You don't have to always *be in* the market. If you just *wait* till PA gets to where you need it to be for you to get what you want *you'll get what you want*. Let the market do all the heavy lifting for you. Only do what you know to be true when working in the live market.

The value areas are quite easy to spot once you have trained your eye to look at current price action and then look up and left. Spot them, draw your lines accordingly, then *wait* for PA to come back and fill your resting order you have waiting. If you are using an automated strategy which I *strongly* encourage you to do, all you will have to do is sit back and wait to get paid. Finally the best advice I can give you is, always use a stop and **keep your hand off** that damn mouse!!

For high profits only trade when you can get them

To know where the smart money is on the chart is very important because they are the ones who are the liquidity providers in the markets. It only makes sense then to do what they are doing with them instead of trying to do something to act against them. Yet retail traders who are the sheeple of the herd will try to go against the smart money and sell at the bottom of a drop in price action where the smart money is waiting to buy from them. Doing this will cause you to have an unfavorable outcome every time.

Identify when your best trading schedule is. When do you find you do your best trading? During RTH, Asian session, London? If you can determine what time works best for you it can greatly help with your profitability. Only go in the live market you work in when the liquidity providers are providing liquidity.

I strongly encourage you to learn the price action of your chosen instrument(s) of choice intimately and familiarize yourself with the times your market has its best movements. Knowing when the smart money liquidity providers are moving the markets is critical so you can be there to ride along with them and make money while they are doing all the hard work. It doesn't get any better than that!

TIP Only deploy your capital in the live market when the liquidity providers are providing liquidity. One way to see this is you can use the journal as a way to see what times in the market you have been working in that the liquidity providers are providing liquidity as that is the *only* time you should be in the market anyway. There are honestly only a few "sweet spot" times that smart money works in the live market and that is when *you* should be working as well.

Knowing when the smart money liquidity providers are moving the markets is critical so you can be there to ride along with them and make money while they are doing all the hard work. It doesn't get any better than that! Only deploy your capital in the live market when the liquidity providers are providing liquidity, very simple.

Do you want to make money or lose it? The choice is totally yours because as I said it's a business and *YOU* are the boss. No one is making you start this business but you. You must know how you tick (no pun intended) and what type of Forex, stock or futures investing and trading is suitable for your personality. Do you want to be a high profit scalper, intraday trader or a position trader?

You need to know when the liquidity providers are providing liquidity so you can take advantage of their volume and make money with the smart money. You need to know the times that the key data points come out for the specific instruments you desire to work in.

When you have this information and can see it on a live price chart in real time and open a position without hesitation you can make a lot of damn money!

My final advice for beginner traders

The best traders *are the best* because they constantly try to improve themselves. I can't stress enough how important this mindset is in trading. The markets are dynamic, and they will demand the very best of you day in and day out.

To really succeed at trading the financial markets, you need to not only thoroughly understand risk reward, position sizing, and risk amount per trade, you also need to consistently execute each of these aspects of money management in combination with a highly effective yet simple to understand trading strategy like price action and supply and demand principles.

It is one thing to have a plan and practice it on demo it is however entirely another to execute it flawlessly in the live markets with your hard earned real money against the best market participants on the planet. Trading is global so make no mistake and think you are in there by yourself.

There is really no easy way to do it honestly. There is a certain progression of steps *all* new traders must go through to be able to drive their own money train to the bank on a daily basis which I have detailed in the book. The progression of steps is to learn money management, gain a hold on your own psychology, learn to read the price charts of the instruments you choose to work in and finally learn how to quantify real supply and demand in the live market to make your trade decisions from.

There are no short cuts and what I just said to study and learn can take quite a while. It all depends on *you* and how much time and effort you are willing to put in to learn what needs to be known to be a successful market participant. For me it was days, nights, weekends and even some holidays. I just wanted to do it *that* bad. It takes a lot of dedication and time.

The best advice I can give you is not to enter the live market with real money until you are ready. It's really that simple. No one is making you do this business. When you think you are going to try to shortcut it just remember there are sharks with fully loaded revolvers in the live market waiting for you to take that shortcut so they can take all your money.

Remember the smoke and flames coming out of your barbeque because you threw all your money in there and didn't have a rule based plan as to how to work in the live markets where you are in competition with sharks.

Who are the sheeple of the herd and who are the smart money you may be asking? The smart money is the Wall Street Banks, institutions, hedge funds, HFT's and dark pools. They are the liquidity providers and market makers. They are whom you need to be able to see on a price chart if you want to make money in the markets.

The sheeple of the herd as I call them are the unprepared or underprepared retail traders who are in the market without the proper training and education or psychological makeup who get FUBAR (fleeced up beyond account recovery) every day in the live markets. You also need to be able to see *them* on a price chart because you can also make money from *them* as well.

Finally it is all about being organized and disciplined. Successful traders have this down pat. They have developed their trading edge over time and have mastered it and built their trading plan around this edge. Some of these traders even go as far as writing their plan out on paper and keeping it with them at all times.

It takes a lot of time and patience to develop this system and these investors and traders have taken the appropriate amount of time to get it down which in turn has made them into consistently profitable and successful market participants.

Learn not to make these mistakes detailed in this book and you can become a consistently profitable market participant in no time. It takes a lot of hard work however if you are committed to doing this business then the amount of time it takes is not an issue. The market is always going to be there waiting for you. *ALWAYS*!

There are no shortcuts to success in investing and trading. You have to do the time if you want to drive the money train. Go do it!

Brand new traders tend to self-sabotage their own efforts at the beginning of their trading careers and businesses because they had not learned that there is a lot to know and have mastered before one can become successful in this business. There are a lot of different things we can do to improve our trading, but there are also things we can do to sabotage our trading as well. One of those things is not getting or having enough information.

It is my goal in this book to give you the information that can help you right from the start of your new trading business the first day. It is so important for traders to start out right from the beginning because the outcome of not having done so is very expensive and no one likes to or wants to lose money. Unfortunately brand new investors and traders tend to lose almost all of their money on their first try in the markets.

One of the things that happen to new investors and traders when they first get into this business is that they lose some of their money right away. They come into the business with unrealistic expectations about how much money they are going to be able to take out of the markets.

The average brand new investor or trader who does not do the proper education and training right from the start loses twenty one thousand dollars on average in the first three months of live trading and an average of forty five thousand dollars in their first year. That's ugly if you ask me.

Almost all brand new investors and traders make the mistakes in this book when they first start out. Now that you have read this entire book and know what *not to do* you can have a head start to driving your money train to the bank on a daily basis. I encourage you to read to other books in my beginner's series as they detail how to become consistently profitable right from the start of your business.

I recommend you start off slow and build on success. You should study each part of what those new beginner series books talk about in detail separately and *master* each individual process before moving on to the next one. How long will that take? As long as it takes! There is no reason to be in any hurry because the market is there waiting to pay you some money every day.

As I said I like to think of it as a big ATM machine because it is open virtually 24 hours a day seven days a week just about. You just need to have the proper PIN# to get your money out. Do the training and education and do not make these mistakes in this book and you will be well on your way to having your own personal PIN# to make money in the live markets every day. It is all about putting all the probabilities in your favor to attain the lowest risk highest reward highest probability outcomes you can have in the live market when putting you hard earned money to work on a daily basis.

Frequently asked questions

Question: When would I be able to quit my job and trade full time?

Answer: To be very conservative and safe not before your income from your investing and trading matches what you make in your current employment.

Question: What kind of investor or trader should I be?

Answer: Figure out what is going to work best for your personality, lifestyle and capital you have to invest.

Question: What can I do to stack the odds in my favor?

Answer: Do the education time the right way from the first day. Use supply and demand and price action.

Question: How long will it take me to become consistently profitable?

Answer: It varies for everyone. It took me 5 years.

Question: What asset class is best to trade?

Answer: The one you see price action the best in and makes you the most money. This eBook is mainly about Forex though.

Question: How many asset classes should I trade?

Answer: I recommend no more than 3. The human brain can only process so much information at one time.

Question: How much time does it take be become consistently profitable?

Answer: That will depend on how fast you grasp the core principles of this type of supply and demand investing and trading

Question: What is the best time frame to invest and trade from?

Answer: I recommend using a daily chart however the method works on all time frames.

Question: What is the best asset class to use this method on?

Answer: That is the beauty of this type of method it works on any asset class. I like to use it for equities and have also used it for Forex futures, crude oil, gold and natural gas with very good results.

Question: How long does it take to fully know this method?

Answer: If you have no experience at all and are just starting out you can get it fairly easily. It took me about a year because I had to unlearn much of what I had previously learned.

Question: Do you use this in all of your investing and trading decisions?

Answer: Yes I do. I only make decisions based on my quantifying supply and demand and the chart.

Question: Does it work all the time?

Answer: Nothing works 100% of the time and to have that belief is a sure recipe for disaster.

Question: What kind of winning percentage will I have using this method?

Answer: You can actually lose quite a bit and still make a nice living using this method. That's what makes it so great.

Question: What would cause me to lose a trade?

Answer: Any number of mistakes however I have found that if I should take a loss it is most likely due to having seen the value area wrong.

Question: What are HFT and AMM?

Answer: HFT stands for high frequency trading and AMM stands for automated market maker. It is thought that about 70% of the market is traded by these computers now.

Question: Do you offer training in this style of investing and trading?

Answer: I offer private mentoring services for beginning investors and traders have are having problems grasping these methods. Feel free to contact me to find out what is required to get on my schedule.

Question: How long does it take to become consistently profitable enough to trade real money?

Answer: As long as it takes. I always tell my students that they do not need to be in any hurry because the market is always going to be there. There are 250 trading days in a year, so you have plenty of opportunities.

Question: Who is the best broker to use for a demo account?

Answer: I would pick a broker who can offer you a demo that you can practice on for a prolonged period of time. Meaning they will give you an unlimited time to learn to invest and trade on their demo.

Question: What is the bare minimum amount of money I can start trading with in the real markets?

Answer: You could start using as little as a hundred dollars if you were trading micro Forex. This gives you exposure to the live market and can also help you start to develop the psychology needed to move up to trading full lots with a bigger account size.

Question: Which is the best investing and trading forum to join?

Answer: I encourage you to check them all out and get a feel for the kind of investors and traders that are in there. Then choose one that matches your style of investing and trading.

Question: What are the best asset classes to invest and trade in?

Answer: You need to figure out what your goals are for your trading business to answer that. Do you want to make short-term income? Do you want to build up your account balance? Do you want to increase your wealth for the long-term? Figure this out before investing and trading real money.

Question: What is the best time to trade?

Answer: When the liquidity providers are providing liquidity.

Question: Who is the smart money?

Answer: Smart money is the banks, institutions, hedge funds, HFTs and black pools. They are the liquidity providers and market makers. They are whom you need to be able to see on a price chart if you want to make money in the markets.

Question: How do I start a journal?

Answer: You can start a journal at the forum where you are learning and also on your own. It can be a Word file, Excel file or just a plain Notepad file. You can also take screenshots of all your charts and save them to a picture file. Many traders post screenshots of their charts in the forums.

Question: How long did it take for you to feel comfortable working in the live markets with real money?

Answer: Five years.

Question: What markets do you work in?

Answer: I position trade equities and have my own Nano hedge fund. I also manage my own ROTH IRA money.

Disclaimer

This book is for educational purposes only. Futures, options, equities, and spot currency trading have large potential risk and traders should be well-educated before putting real money at risk. You must be aware of the risks and willing to accept them in order to invest in all markets. Never trade with money you can't afford to lose. This book is neither a recommendation, solicitation nor an offer to buy/sell a futures contract or currency.

Forex, futures, stock, and options trading is not appropriate for everyone. There is a substantial risk of loss associated with trading these markets. Losses can and will occur. No system or methodology has ever been developed that can guarantee profits or ensure freedom from losses. No representation or implication is being made that using the trading concepts, methodology or system or the information in this book will generate profits or ensure freedom from losses.

HYPOTHETICAL OR SIMULATED PERFORMANCE RESULTS HAVE CERTAIN LIMITATIONS. UNLIKE AN ACTUAL PERFORMANCE RECORD, SIMULATED RESULTS DO NOT REPRESENT ACTUAL TRADING. ALSO, SINCE THE TRADES HAVE NOT BEEN EXECUTED, THE RESULTS MAY HAVE UNDER-OR-OVER COMPENSATED FOR THE IMPACT, IF ANY, OF CERTAIN MARKET FACTORS, SUCH AS LACK OF LIQUIDITY. SIMULATED TRADING PROGRAMS IN GENERAL ARE ALSO SUBJECT TO THE FACT THAT THEY ARE DESIGNED WITH THE BENEFIT OF HINDSIGHT. NO REPRESENTATION IS BEING MADE THAT ANY ACCOUNT WILL OR IS LIKELY TO ACHIEVE PROFIT OR LOSSES SIMILAR TO THOSE SHOWN.